W9-ARF-109

Step-by-Step Transformations

Turning Apples into Applesauce

Wendy A. Reynolds

Cavendish Square

New York

For my daughter, Dashiell, who's learning, step by step.

Published in 2016 by Cavendish Square Publishing, LLC
243 5th Avenue, Suite 136, New York, NY 10016

First Edition

Website: cavendishsq.com

This publication represents the opinions and views of the author based on his or her personal experience, knowledge, and research. The information in this book serves as a general guide only. The author and publisher have used their best efforts in preparing this book and disclaim liability rising directly or indirectly from the use and application of this book.

CPSIA Compliance Information: Batch #WS15CSQ

All websites were available and accurate when this book was sent to press.

Library of Congress Cataloging-in-Publication Data

Reynolds, Wendy A., author.
Turning apples into applesauce / Wendy A. Reynolds.
pages cm. — (Step-by-step transformations)
Includes bibliographical references and index.
ISBN 978-1-50260-443-9 (hardcover) ISBN 978-1-50260-442-2 (paperback) ISBN 978-1-50260-444-6 (ebook)
1. Applesauce—Juvenile literature. 2. Cooking (Apples)—Juvenile literature. I. Title.

TX813.A6R395 2016
641.6'411—dc23

2014049218

Editorial Director: David McNamara
Copy Editor: Rebecca Rohan
Art Director: Jeffrey Talbot
Designer: Alan Sliwinski
Senior Production Manager: Jennifer Ryder-Talbot
Production Editor: Renni Johnson

Photos by: National Geographic/Getty Images, cover; Ildi Papp/Shutterstock.com, cover; © iStockphoto.com/philipimage, 5; James Braund/Photolibrary/Getty Images, 7; Todd Gipstein/National Geographic/Getty Images, 9; Alistair Berg/Digital Vision/Getty Images, 11; Photo Courtesy of Musselman's, 13, 15, 17, 19; Ildi Papp/Shutterstock.com, 21.

Printed in the United States of America

Contents

Applesauce is made
from apples.

5

Apples are picked from the apple trees.

7

They are taken to the **factory** in trucks and unloaded.

Workers sort the apples.

Apples that are **rotten** are thrown away.

Now, machines peel the apples to remove their skin.

The **core** and **seeds** are taken out.

13

The peeled apples are cut and chopped.

15

The chopped apples are put into a large pot called a **kettle**.

They are cooked until the apples are soft.

The applesauce is poured into jars to be sold.

18

19

Applesauce is a sweet, **healthy** treat!

21

New Words

factory (FAK-tor-ee) A building where products are made.

healthy (HELL-thee) Good for your body.

kettle (KEH-tel) A container used for heating or boiling.

rotten (ROH-ten) When food is too old to use or eat.

seeds (SEEDS) A small object from a plant from which a new plant will grow.

Index

About the Author

Writer, editor, and educator **Wendy Reynolds** loves to make homemade applesauce every fall with her husband and daughter in their home in Orlando, Florida.

About BOOK WORMS

Bookworms help independent readers gain reading confidence through high-frequency words, simple sentences, and strong picture/text support. Each book explores a concept that helps children relate what they read to the world in which they live.